Adrift on a Sea
of
Shadows

a collection of poetry

Adrift on a Sea of Shadows

a collection of poetry

SPYDER COLLINS

QUILL & CROW PUBLISHING HOUSE

ADRIFT ON A SEA OF SHADOWS BY SPYDER COLLINS
PUBLISHED BY QUILL & CROW PUBLISHING HOUSE

Designed by Lauren Hellekson

Printed in the United States of America

ISBN 978-1-7356863-4-9

Author's Website: https://spydercollins.carrd.co

Traverse the waves that make up my soul
Know where I rise and where I fall
Forever lifting me, just to let me go
Pull me from the shadows, push me into corners

Hidden in your insecurities
Through it all
Angst
Pain
Wanting

Traverse the chambers that make up my heart
Listening to the rhythm as it beats
Echoes of Sorrow and Loneliness
Tug at it and you will undestand

It beats only for
... you.

Demon nips at me
Sins I sleep with
In my Field of Reeds
Days are night
Nights are night
Life in darkness
Sins that slither
Through my veins
For I am nothing
Never being, vapor
Solitude as I lay
Supine in my field
This is my burden
Loneliness beneath
Aquamarine skies.

My skin splits
Division
My blood boils
Malice

I can feel you
In my veins
I can taste you
On my tongue

My bones break
Tension
My marrow leaks
Affliction

I CAN TASTE HER ON MY FINGERTIPS, HER SKIN UNDER
MY FINGERNAILS. I NIBBLE AT THEM LIKE AN ANXIOUS
BRIDE. THE LOOK IN HER EYES STILL REGISTERS WITH ME.
AS HER LIFE DRAINED INTO MY HANDS. MY MANICURED
NAILS PUSHED INTO HER THROAT. I COULD FEEL HER
DYING BREATH AS IT SLIPPED OVER MY FINGERS. YOUR
SOUL IS A DEBT COLLECTED.

Death comes and I am grateful
This misery drains my essence
Please stay by my side as I wander
The journey will be short, I promise.

Horned God is silent
Nightshade calls for the Sorrow
Leaf about my soul
Blood moon rises, death follows
To soothe a soul forsaken.

In decay
I cherish
A drink
Of fatality.

I rot
Open cavity
This loam
Devours me.

Raven picks
At carrion
I smile
Death lingers.

Away now
Raven flies
Heart held
Talons grip.

Long goodbyes
Short cries
Next life
Is forever.

You are everything to me.
The unattainable dream,
the secret no one told,
and the life no one lived.
Your name catches in my throat,
and the tears build inside of me.
You are forever lost in my memory.

Lips as dark as Raven's coat
Her eyes are flecks of gold
Lost in a sea of aquamarine
The air about her, brooding, yet inviting
Absorbed in her torment and pain,
My everything sewn into a dream.

She is my muse, drawing on my sorrow
A lamplight in the still, utter darkness
Selfless gift of inspiration
My heart flutters about her, dreaming
I hold what I have, more I will never know
Accepting upon these threads of hope.

I don't want this to be me
Sorrow in a bag of bones
My heart sewn on a sleeve
But what can I do, really
Hidden in the shadow of this
Loneliness.

I swear I won't let this define me
Choking on my own promises
Wanting to be let in
But troubled by the pain it may bring
So, I wander along the shore of this
Despair.

Pain grows within like ivy
Spreading and clinging to all of me
I fight against who I am
But never do I win
Holding my eyes closed against this
Pain.

Hold me, I ask from the emptiness
That is me.

I pray at the altar of you.
Peel back my skin,
one layer at a time.
Remove my eyelids
to never miss the sight of you.
Rip out my heart
to show my adoration
through pain.
It just never seems to be enough.
So I will slip back into this hole,
and say goodbye.

HER CANVAS LAYS NICELY OVER MINE. THE BLOOD WARMS MY SKIN, AND THE SMELL SOOTHES ME. THE ART WAS PAINSTAKING, BUT WELL WORTH THE OUTCOME. I WALK AS HER NOW, BUT WITH MY THOUGHTS AND AN APPRECIATION FOR MY TALENTS, SHE NEVER SHOWED.

⌐

How sorrow does sting
Like frozen rain against bare skin
Biting at each moment
A pain a needle could cure.

I sit contemplating my demise
Needle inches from my vein
Would it matter if I died?
Understanding fully that it wouldn't.

The needle dangles from my vein
A spoonful did it sip
The warmth rushes through me
Eyes heavy and finally,
I am free.

To drink from your lips
and indulge in your perfect curves
to feel the warmth of your embrace
and to get lost in all of you.

The fragrant smell of you, Sinful
The feel of your skin, Seductive
How you love beneath me, Tempting
And the taste of you, Delectable.

My love ...

Perfection in mind, soul, and flesh
All of this you were
But in death, violent, and fresh
Your body I did take
And what a meal
You will make.

ANTIQUE EYES STARE AT ME. HELL NIPS AT MY EAR,
WHISPERING TO FALL INTO THE ABYSS. I DRAW A BLADE
UPWARD. COMFORTABLE NOW IN MEMORIES OF YOU.
THOUGHTS DIMINISH, AND DARKNESS INVITES ITSELF IN.
BREATHS SHALLOW. I CAN GO HOME NOW TO THE FLAMES
THAT CALL FOR MY SOUL.

If love was a canvas,
I'd paint on it every day
Landscapes of you and me
And darkness along the way.

My brush fashioned
Of your ribs and hair
Your skull as my palette
Painting love in a nightmare.

Now that I have you
I will never let you go
In my gore dreams you will stay
In pieces as you are stowed.

Scant cobwebs and smoke
I never wanted to be
In the light, I drown
Shadows no longer conceal
I put death on like a coat

... and I wait.

I used a can opener
to dislodge my sternum,
pulled my rib cage open,
and gave you my heart.

Hypnotic hands reach for me. Black Dahlia smiles (as if she has a choice). I reach out to touch her, wanting to feel her pale skin.

"I am a collector of pretty things," I say, but I never can.

Everything I touch disappears.

⌐⍁

My, your verdant eyes
They are filled with such mercy
How they beguile me
Lost in a meadow with you
Forever beneath the moon.

Bloodworms swim in my eyes,
maggots crawl through my skin.
My organs are liquifying,
and I am decaying from within.

These days how they labor,
only insatiable insects with me.
Screams of my flesh being eaten,
is my only real company.

Here I lie, immobile and stiff,
waiting for flesh to turn to bone.
Decades I will wait for collagen,
before my soul may return home.

Wraith peers at Raven
Her wings part, inviting
He sinks into her, biting
At the very heart of Raven.

Raven walks with Wraith
Past the darkness, divination
And ominous shadows, invocation
At the very soul of Wraith.

Wraith and Raven journey
As ghosts along a path, unknown
Never truly as one, alone
At the very core of their journey.

LONELINESS GROWS THROUGH MY FLESH LIKE IVY. CREEPING
DOWN MY SPINE AND WRAPPING ITS TENDRILS AROUND MY
HEART. TIGHTLY IT SQUEEZES, MY BLOOD OOZES FROM
WITHIN, DROWNING ME IN SORROW.
I AM ROOTED NOW, AND HERE I WILL REMAIN.

I will be forgotten
as a wisp of memory,
like a pappus in the wind
here today and gone tomorrow.

I will be forgotten
a shadow of a thought,
or the name not remembered
the word on the tip of your tongue.

As I slip from you
and the days bleed on,
I dissolve with lost memories,
nothing more than a web in a dream.

A web runs through me
Simple threads of emotion
Some tug at my heart
While others pull at my rage
I've puncture scars
Where I've tried to sever the web
To no avail.

This web pulls deeply and hard
Simple threads of sorrow
Strangle and dig into my heart
They suffocate me now
This simple web entangles my soul
I'm not fighting any longer
Pull the veil.

She wears Death's dress
Sprinkles tears of blood
Trickling down her cheeks
Timeless she is
My maiden,
Fatality.

I'm not afraid of dying
We all get the call
Her hands are cold but soft
Comforting she is
My maiden,
Mortality.

As I walk this path
She says the fields are forgiving
I am at ease, this death
Reassuring she is
My maiden,
Finality.

BUTTON EYES AND A HAND-DRAWN MOUTH. BURLAP SKIN
AND HAND-SEWN CLOTHING. IT HAS NO HANDS, SO IT
CANNOT HOLD ME. IT HAS NO FEET, SO IT CANNOT FLEE.
NOR CAN IT LISTEN OR SPEAK, FOR THAT MATTER. IT DOES,
HOWEVER, HOLD YOUR HEART
IN ITS CHEST.

⤙

She holds my strings
Pulling them as she pleases
She has already clipped my wings,
Now it's my heart she teases.

It's the slow telling sigh,
that look in her eye,
the curl of her lip,
and the sway of her hip.

It's her breath upon my ear,
the whisper only I can hear,
a graze of a finger tip,
and her gentle grip.

It's the build before the end,
a feeling only she can transcend,
the still before the fire,
set my soul adrift upon the pyre.

There is a forest in my mind,
trees are arms stretching to the sky.
Crooked fingers reaching,
seeking perhaps a simple reply.

They tear at the air,
returning nothing more than despair.
Tiring over time,
they falter in my mind, but I don't care.

I feel it all going away,
I can feel it slipping in my mind.
Crawling away, like a spider,
leaving all but my sanity behind.

THESE SCARS TELL MY TALE. THEY RUN TO THE BONE. YOU
WILL NEED TO SKIN ME TO READ ME. EACH LAYER, LIKE RINGS
ON A TREE. IF YOU CAN MAKE IT THROUGH MY STORY, I WILL
GRANT YOU A SINGLE WISH. BUT YOU FIRST MUST SEW ME
BACK TOGETHER AGAIN.

Heartache rides the waves of the sea.
My love tossed about with the debris.
How the waves roll and crash o'er me.
Tearing flesh from bone, this lustful sea.

I have such a love for this glorious sea.
A truth you knew and used against me.
Taking me to its depths now, a Siren's plea.
Death beneath a tempestuous sea.

The darkness bleeds from my eyes.
Light succumbs, then fades and dies.
Your hate is telling, like little notes.
Wish I'd sink, my emptiness floats.

My hollow heart holds no intentions.
A pointless soul, without ambition.
I am broken, so how can I feel
A lost dream that was never real.

I love the ash of the dead
How it plays in the wind
Or feels between my fingers
The ashen tint it holds
and a smell so brute
I would fill a sandbox
To build castles of ash
This ash brings me joy
This ash of the dead.

NEMESIS TOWERS ABOVE HUMANITY. HER FORCE SHOWS IN HER MANNER, AND HER AVIDITY RESTS IN HER EYES. STARS OF ANTIQUITY SWIRL ABOUT HER HAND. THE TIP OF HER SWORD POINTS TO THE HEART OF MANKIND. IN HER BATTLE GEAR, SHE AWAITS THE WORD FROM NYX. HUBRIS FROM AN UNTHANKFUL AND UNTHINKING BROOD DRAWS RETRIBUTION. NEMESIS HOLDS TIME, AND MORTALITY IS FLEETING.

As I walk through a dream,
I find it is not my own.
A dream so inviting it's captive,
but as I go, I find I am alone.
A secret love brews in darkness,
one I can feel as if my own.
But when this dream lifts,
I wake to find, that I am still alone.

I can never be,
more than nothing.
A hollow feeling,
that lingers, at best.
When I am here,
I bring not a thought.
When I am gone,
I am easily forgotten.
As I say farewell,
you will not in kind.
Because I am truly,
Nothing.

I feel the stab of loneliness once again.
The cords that weaved our spirits together are no more.
Sorrow falls from me like a mourning rain.
There is an emptiness I cannot elude, inure evermore.

I hold out my hand to you, returning empty.
Calls to the ethereal shrouded by my drowning pain.
I ponder now, as the heartache grows in me.
Does any part of what we weaved remain?

HEKATE RETREATS AS AURORA APPROACHES. LUNA SINKS BEHIND THE VEIL. THE TWILIGHT BOWS TO EOS AS THE NIGHT SUCCUMBS TO THE DAY. IN HER STAY AMONG THE LUNAR SHEETS AND WHISPERS OF MAGIC, SHE FINDS PEACE ON THE SHORES OF INFINITY. THE LUNAR WAVES REFLECT GENERATIONS OF NECROMANCY, AS SPECTERS DRIFT ABOUT THEIR MOTHER. THIS GODDESS HEKATE IS THE NIGHT AND THE HANGING MOON BUT BEWARE THE HINT OF DARKNESS THAT FLOATS ABOUT HER. FOR THOSE WHO TEST HER WILL KNOW THE HASTE OF A GODDESS SCORNED.

Wraith took a blade,
stuck it in his chest,
and scraped against
his ribcage.
Like a violin he played
...
a somber tune.

Her touch is like stardust at twilight.
The scent of petrichor floats about her.
Her eyes draw me to boundless seas.
Arms bring the warmth of a winter's fire.

I can taste forever on her wet lips.
Feel the beating heart of eternity upon her thigh.
My eyes take in the glory of a Goddess.
In her sigh, I hear the very voice of Creation.

.

The daughters of Nyx,
of Fate and timely tricks.
Spinner of webs so frail,
life measured on a scale.
A line drawn at birth,
deciding life's length and worth.
Death cut by golden shears,
mortality veiled behind falling tears.

THE NYMPH FELL TO SLUMBER, BOUND TO HER DREAMS
THAT WEAVE BETWEEN THE BEATS OF HER HEART. A
VESTAL SOUL IS SHE, WITH THOUGHTS SO INNOCENT AND
TELLING. THE LAND OF DREAMS SHE APPROACHES, SEA-
GIRT, AND A SAIL. SAND SPRINKLES OVER HER SLEEPING
EYES. ABOVE HER, A BATTLE OF WILLS ENSUES. MORPHEUS
SPELLS BACK PHOBETOR TO BRING THE NYMPH DREAMS
AS PURE AS SHE, I. INSTEAD OF THE ILLICIT MARE THAT
WOULD HAVE BEFALLEN HER. AGAIN THIS NIGHT, HER SOUL
REMAINS UNSULLIED, AND THE LAVE OF CALM
IS HER ʿSCAPE.

A tangled web,
of heart strings
and dreams.

Cut a cord,
and then they
become two.

Tug the heart,
it bursts at
the seams.

Madness in my pedigree.
Hate embedded in my DNA.
A bloodline of miscreants.

I am what you fear most,
I am you.

Preying on the innocent.
Artifice stitched into your fiber.
You are the human condition.

You are what I fear most,
You are you.

When darkness pushes me
to the edge of ruin.
When loneliness cuts a hole
into my beating heart.
When pain bores through me
to the edge of a blade.
When regret teases at an end
always tearing me apart.

I stop and I think of her
raven hair so fine
skin as soft as silk
eyes of passionate seas
lips tempting me.

In her I find a peace
a place to curl up and be
boundless stars and inviting seas
warmth and a place to be at ease.
In her I find my eternity

I SIP OF YOU, FROM A CUP. MADE OF BONE, HAIR, AND LEATHERED FLESH. ANOTHER REMNANT OF THE LOVE WE SHARED. OUR TORRID, PASSIONATE, AND RECKLESS AFFAIR.

I will swallow you whole,
spit out the pits and save your soul.
Scars are carved into your skin,
tomes that define the extent of your sin.
The depths of hell await us all,
penance served under the Devil's thrall.
Come now to your fiery end,
as I have many more souls to tend.

When you don't deserve happiness
What do you do each morning
As painful it is to wake, somehow you do
Though loneliness follows you
You walk your path looking for someone
A companion to share some joy
But the path is empty, then you remember
You don't deserve happiness.

This scar I carry,
is a relic of you
A lovely sin,
of a time forgotten
Seasons change,
but the heart lingers
And so do
my memories of you.

Do what you do best
Stripping the flesh from my bones
Why is love deadly?

I lay here,
lost among ancient words,
roaming among the shores,
wanting the impossible,
and forever one with the endless night.

Apart from my fate
In death I cannot hate
Blisters blind me
I can no longer see.

I BRING YOU TO MY LIPS. LIKE IN LIFE, YOUR HEART IS VOID OF SUBSTANCE AND TASTELESS. I SWEAR IT FLUTTERED AS I BIT INTO IT. PERHAPS IT WAS JUST MY HEART, FILLED WITH JOY.

She tugs at my heart
Before she tears it apart
Threads of hope fade
As dreams are frayed.

I am imprisoned in my own heart
Feeling blackened and bare
From a life and love torn apart.

Though I try, I can never be
Anything more than a ghost of me
Take me as I am or leave me be
Set me afloat on an unaccompanied sea
Bits and parts are all you will see
Is it enough to keep you here with me?

Remembrance of life
kicking ashes under foot
I walk on your grave.

BLOOD FLOWS FREELY FROM A SEVERED THROAT. LIFE
LABORS UNDER DEATH'S GRIP. A BODY CRUMBLES TO THE
FLOOR IN MOVEMENTS THAT MIMIC A MARIONETTE. DEATH
BRINGS A LONG SMILE TO ACCOMPANY THE SILENCE.

Everything that is me is blackened
Only space grows in this isolation
I can no longer bear this one that is me
Thoughts of death glisten like stars
Do I have it in me to let this all go?
Memories of a past love burdens me
without you.

Fingers once again in my veins
The hot fluid skitters about me
I sink into the floor and feel
For the first time without pain
Take me with you, under your wing
Don't leave me here to wake,
without you.

On the path of dread
And atop the knoll of pain
Among the reeds
You will find my beating heart
Sorrow brought me here, to die.

In a shallow grave,
I lay.
Bones broken,
skin fissured,
organs exposed

In a shallow grave
I decay.
I am fodder,
a hovel,
and litter.

In a shallow grave
I lay.
Finally useful,
Without delay.

I give back,
as I decay.
In this shallow grave,
where I lay.

This dark creature
How it haunts my every eve
It gnaws at me
Claws at thoughts
Grips my heart
And licks my very soul
This demon, this mare
Of lore or myth, you say
Then I invite you
Come
Come
to my nightmare
You will see
the mære of my dreams.

Misery rides me
like a child on a pony
round and round I go.

I AM NOT SICK, NOT AT ALL. I HAVE A PINING FOR BLOOD. THE WARMTH IT HAS ON THE SKIN. IT TICKLES, AS IT MAKES ITS WAY. THE BRIGHT CRIMSON AROUSES, AND NO LESS DOES MY WANTING DEATH. OH, BUT NOT JUST YET. THIS CIRCUS IS MY AFFAIR, AND I WILL GO ON UNTIL I CAN NO MORE.

The fragrant forest
covers the stench of decay
of the flesh I lay.

Moving through muscle fibers
soaking in her blood,
Pushing veins and arteries
aside like cobwebs

Drilling into bones
feasting on marrow,
Weaving through hollow bone
making way to her core

Here I will make my home
rhythmic beat my comfort.
You can find me hanging from a web
in the chambers of her heart.

A random pocket
Holds your blood and ashes
A part of me now.

HADES SPIT THE SOUL OF ETERNITY FROM HIS LUNGS. THE WALL OF HUMANITY WILTS UNDER ITS BURDEN. SOLACE WEEPS TO RAPTURE AS HADES RISES FROM THE LAKE OF FIRE. IT IS NOW HIS TIME AND, IN HIS WAKE, SALVATION TREMBLES.

I am beholden to you, stark darkness and dread.
In my hand, I hold a doll made of her skin and hair.
It is a lovely doll, supple and fair, much like her.
But her affections she would not give, so I took them.
To you, I offer my soul, just so I can have her always.

The ocean calls to my content,
Breakers crash over my grief,
The sway eases my discontent,
In the salty smell of the ocean, belief.

Now that my web of despair is gone,
On the shore, they will find my body come dawn.

Rights to the nefarious
Incantations serenade the damned.
Tenants of lost souls
Undeniable are the forlorn
Allegory of the wanting.
Longings of the forsaken

Discover more from this author at
www.quillandcrowpublishinghouse.com

Made in the USA
Middletown, DE
19 March 2021